THE ASSISTANT'S HANDBOOK

PRINCIPLES FOR SUCCESS IN THE ENTERTAINMENT INDUSTRY

ANDRES B. COPELAND

THE ASSISTANT HANDBOOK

Principles For Success In The Entertainment Industry

Copyright © 2019 by Andres B. Copeland

ISBN:

Cover Design and Interior by AugustPride, LLC

ILLUMINATION PRESS 1100 Peachtree Street, Suite 250 Atlanta, Georgia 30309 United States InspirationalAuthors.com

THIS BOOK IS DEDICATED TO
DERRICK D'ANDRE JONES

TABLE OF CONTENTS

THE JOURNEY

My passion for cutting hair sparked the year I turned thirteen. Until then, my father was my barber. Because my mother was often sick and suffering from sickle cell anemia, my father became a jack of all trades. He took over many household duties, including being the family's hairstylist. Each week, we experienced a new side of creativity and determination from my father, as he cut my hair and braided my sisters' hair.

My father took on more responsibility over the years, becoming the sole bread winner of the family. Soon, he became too busy to continue as our hairstylist. As a result, I took matters into my own hands and decided I would start cutting my own hair. With my mother's guidance, I cut my hair for the first time at our kitchen table. I thought the experience went well and felt very accomplished. Feeling confident I had done a great job; I could not wait to show my friends.

Unfortunately, my friends were not at all impressed. In fact, the first person to who I showed my new haircut suggested never attempting to cut my own hair ever again. While I was a bit deflated, I was still determined.

Most of my friends and classmates went to Capital Cuts, the premiere barber shop in Hampton Roads, Virginia. Each week, they would come to school with fresh new cuts. I admired and studied their styles while determining how I could re-create them for myself. After several attempts, I was able to cut in a variety of styles. It wasn't long before my skills were much better. Now, my friends asked me to cut their hair. It was a big win for me, especially since my friends had discouraged me from attempting to cut my own hair in the beginning.

As I became more proficient, my confidence and passion for cutting hair grew. I went from cutting my friends' hair in my kitchen to cutting my friends' and roommates' hair in my dorm room at Longwood University. I dreamed of eventually going to cosmetology school, and pursuing my dream career. Although, I didn't know how to make it happen. I had a great passion, but there was not a clear path.

After struggling in college for almost three years, I became tired of spinning my wheels. Cutting hair as a side hustle was great, but I knew that I wasn't heading in the direction which I wanted to go. I was feeling pressure to "get serious and figure it all out." After all, having a dream was great, but what I really needed was a way to make a living, right?

That's when I decided to join the U.S. Navy. My first duty station was in San Diego aboard the USS Vincennes (CG-49). I gave my all to my duties, taking on whatever opportunities were presented. But, in the back of my mind, I still held my desire to cut hair. My desire was so strong that I could not hide it. Soon my passion—and skills—were discovered. With more than four hundred shipmates on board, I stayed pretty busy cutting hair. This only fanned the flames of my desire even more. I was determined to find a way to open up my own barber shop.

It took me ten years, but on my thirtieth birthday, I finally committed to pursuing my passion full-time. I went to cosmetology school in Wheaton, Maryland to earn my barbering license. At the time, I thought owning a barber shop would be my highest dream. But then...I saw "The Blow Out." This reality television show followed the life of Jonathan Antin, a Beverly Hills salon owner whose clientele included some of Hollywood's biggest celebrities.

After watching that show, my dream expanded. My barber shop dreams now seemed too small for me. I had stars in my eyes. Knowing I could become a celebrity stylist was my ultimate goal. But, once again, I ran into a challenge. How was I supposed to make my dream a reality?

My first strategy was completing research online. Unfortunately, Google was not any help. As soon as I earned my barbering license in Maryland, I decided to move to Los Angeles to figure it out for myself.

In 2006, I arrived in California without any contacts and very few resources. But, I made up for that lack with my relentless hope and determination. Single-mindedly focused, I promised myself I would keep pressing until I reached my goals. Within the first two weeks after arriving in California, I made a list of the top fifty salons in Los Angeles. I set out to find a job that would provide me with the best training possible.

Before applying to a salon, I first visited it to check out its vibe. Making sure I was working in a comfortable, positive environment was a top priority for me.

My first job was in West Hollywood at the Warren-Tricomi Salon where I assisted the talented Eric Johnson. As I watched

Eric work, I learned a lot about passion and persistence. I realized skill and talent are necessary, but without passion, you won't get very far. I additionally learned there are some other key ingredients to success which are not always obvious or taught.

Persist Until You Succeed

Once I moved to Los Angeles, I had an idea of what I wanted to accomplish for myself. I also had a timeline for my goals. Believing I was well on my way to landing my first job, six months later I received a letter that stopped me in my tracks. Although I had passed the exams and requirements for licensing in Maryland, that licensing did not transfer to California. If I didn't get my license in California, I wouldn't be able to work anymore.

I was devastated. I didn't have the money to go to cosmetology school in California, so I had to find a way to pass the exams. Therefore, I could meet California's requirements another way. It took me three state board exams and 3,600 hours of apprenticeship assisting at John Frieda to get my California license.

Persistence is your willingness to not only see your success, but to see what obstacles come your way.

Your perspective on your current situation determines its outcome. It is important to take everything that happens—good or bad—as an opportunity to learn and grow. This is the mindset that helped me to press on when it seemed as if all the odds were against me. Yes, I had to start my licensing from scratch and take what appeared to be a step back. However, I wasn't willing to give up.

Take The Risk

Early in my journey, a close friend gave me a powerful book—"The Alchemist" by Paulo Coelho. The most impactful lesson I received from this book was this: don't be afraid to live and take risks.

It's always easy to find reasons why you shouldn't go after your dreams. Not enough education...not enough money... not enough time...too many other responsibilities...

If I gave you a few minutes, you could probably fill an entire page with reasons as to why you can't go after the life and dreams you really want right now. But, if I asked you to write all the reasons why you should go after your dreams, most people draw a blank. That's because you know that going after what you really want will cause you to have to give up some things. You will have to give up your fears and insecurities. You will have to give up your comfort zone. You may have to give up some friends.

It's a big risk to go after your dreams. But, in the end what, you have to give up cannot even compare to what you will gain.

There Is No Plan B

My only option was to reach my goal. I didn't have a backup plan. I didn't even consider what would happen if I failed. My focus was totally concentrated on my success. There were times when this was very hard to do.

Six months after arriving in Los Angeles (around the same time I discovered I would have to start all over with my licensing), I experienced a devastating professional loss. One day, after spending a few fun hours with my daughter at the beach, I discovered my car had been broken into. Inside of my car was my entire professional kit. The tools I needed to work were gone. Now, not only was I trying to figure out a way to earn my California license and keep my job, but I also had to find a way to replace the tools I'd lost.

For a brief moment, I faltered. Was this a sign that I was on the wrong track?

But those thoughts only lasted for a moment. I reminded myself of my passion and dreams. I focused on my end goal, and was determined to keep going. I was fortunate to get support from a loved one whom replaced my kit. I believe it was my no-plan-B attitude that helped me through this situation. Every plan needs a contingency—except when it comes to your passion and goals.

When you split your focus between things going right and/or things going wrong, you can easily be swayed to get off track.

Every time an obstacle or challenge comes up, you'll become disheartened. Your mind will be filled with the "what if it doesn't happen" scenarios. But, if you have only one option, you'll be able to see the obstacles and challenges as what they really are—stepping stones to your goal.

Nonetheless, remember this—while you plan a (goal, dream, or vision) should never change. Sometimes the path you travel to get there will. Keep your GPS pointed to your final destination but be willing to be rerouted from time to time along the way. In the end, if you stay true to your course, you'll arrive at your goal.

AWARENESS

When I first arrived in California, I was extremely green to be working in a high-profile salon. I hadn't any idea what I was doing, but I had a clear understanding of what goals I wanted to accomplish.

As an ex-military/federal contractor with a background in barbering, my first point of entry into the industry was Google. I did extensive searches on, "how to become a celebrity hairstylist." To my dismay, I found there were not any stated or written rules for navigating through a career in this industry. There weren't any books on how to win over senior stylists willing to train you. There were not any guides to teach you how to handle the long work hours or how to find the miracle in each day. I had to essentially depend on my own levels of awareness, while gaining an understanding of the new culture into which I was starting.

I learned how to be observant of my surroundings.

It's important to see as many details about your environment as possible. This was a lesson my father exposed me to at a young age. Look beyond what you can see at first glance. Search for more with your eyes and be visually curious.

In the beginning, being aware of the way people communicated and functioned in the salon setting was a steep learning curve. However, I brought my military attention to detail and my gratitude to being there. I became aware of people's behaviors and the verbal games which happened in a salon. I used these skills as I started assisting customers, understanding that knowing the details allows you to deal with things that come up in any circumstance.

As an assistant, you are working with someone to make things flow smoothly. Knowing as many details as possible could aid in your performance. There's a level of compassion regarding how detailed you are to the client and the stylist's needs. Here are a few things to keep in mind while building your awareness muscles—

Think with your heart and go the extra mile.

Whether it's researching information for the stylist, verbally checking that the stylist doesn't need anything, or being intuitive to the process–you can always find ways to make things easier.

Take the Initiative

After you understand your duties and the project's priorities, it's go time. It's time to prove that you appreciate the opportunity given to you by doing your best work.

You are responsible for the task given; so, always work as if there is no time to waste. There's not. People are depending on you to make the service seamless, regardless of the circumstance. In any work-flow relationship, it naturally takes time for that to be created. But even in your first time working with someone, be aggressive in being helpful.

For example, you may get to the job early and see there're some key components that are not in place. It is your duty to find a solution. Use your awareness to ensure the person you are assisting has everything necessary for the day--power sergers, wind machine, extension cords, appliances, and any other essential tool. As a professional, you'll know what is needed to complete a task or day's work.

Use every moment available.

I was once told by hairstylist, Ashley Javier, "Idle hands are the devil's work."

When you're standing around not being productive, you can and will be bored. This is when the discipline is broken. When your discipline is broken, you've lost your focus. There are so many variables on which your attention needs to be focused for it to be completely supportive.

I have lived by this motto for years: "If you've time to lean, there's time to clean." I think this was something from my past military journey that stuck with me.

Another that is pure gold: "If you stay ready, you won't have to get ready." Coach Joe Langston taught me that at IC Norcom High School.

Being on set, you always have to be ready in every way. Decisions and/or the creative direction could change; however, your focus is to be prepared to handle this workflow.

Understanding of your position and what you want out of it

We are all given opportunities—opportunities for a better career; opportunities for better networking; opportunities for another opportunity. Though when the opportunities come knocking, will you be ready to open the door?

You never know when it is coming. An opportunity comes to us and we are unclear on what we want out of that experience. So, we don't create the focused intention required to receive it. If you are not ready when your opportunity comes, the opportunity will pass you by. As an assistant, you are in an incredible position. It's up to you to create the plan that helps you make the most of it.

When I started assisting, I understood that there was a game and dance which had to be played. Consequently, I choose to see through the surface issues and focus on my challenge at hand.

With each opportunity, my intentions were set on making this a positive experience which would lead me to the next opportunity.

I'd take extra pride in every task, whether it was folding towels or shampooing a client. I wanted to leave the impression I was a hard worker and that I belonged there.

Knowing what I wanted out of any opportunity has helped me not get caught up in the things with which I may not agree. This focus allowed me to look past my ego and accomplish the goal. I was therefore able to deliver the best quality of service, all the while satisfying my personal goals for my life.

I wasn't deterred by the obstacles in my journey. No matter what happened or what direction I chose, I was clear on where I was in the journey. I wanted to learn and develop my skills from these experiences. I was committed to being a hair assistant. Moreover, I worked and learned from the top hairstylists in the industry.

There were moments I couldn't allow my own frustration to get into the way of my experience. My ego/insecurity would've loved to get in the way, and it would have—should I let some things become personal.

We all have good days and bad days, but my attitude was: my bad days are also my good days, while my good days are great days. I knew that I was fortunate to live my dream. Rain or shine, I was going to go for it. Even in my worst moments, whether it was relationship-related or job insecurities, I picked myself up to see what was next on the journey. One thing which really helped me stay focused was setting my intentions by writing them down and declaring them every day.

Don't let your ego get in the way. When I decided to take my hairstylist experience seriously, I felt as if I had to be honest with myself. I had to be willing to put my egotistical hang ups to the side, so that I could advance and experience more. I committed myself to the experience of making the person I was assisting look good professionally. I was dedicated to improving my experience with them, all while learning their processes. Additionally, I wanted to sharpen my game and see where this focus would take me. I was open to working every job, with minimal talking, maximum listening, and continuous learning.

Keep It Moving! Left Foot...Right Foot...Left Foot...

There'll be times on your journey when you question whether you should continue. Even with all of your awareness, things happen beyond your control. These threaten to knock you off course. After losing my first job at Warren-Tricomi, I wasn't sure about the next salon opportunity. I shopped my résumé around and showed my interest in several salons.

Unfortunately, full-time work was not available. At first, I panicked and immediately thought of going back to my roots of barbering. Staring at Craigslist listings for beauty gigs, I told myself that this was temporary; only until I get into the salon of my choice. After two months of barbering at New Millennial on Wilshire Boulevard, I saw my dream job come available. Packing my things, I never looked back.

I walked into John Frieda Salon and interviewed, securing an assistant position that lasted the next three years.

Keep your purpose in front of you and be willing to pivot.

Knowing your purpose and what you want will help you determine when to change your direction. Sometimes circumstances change and no longer align with your purpose. Your awareness to see the changes around you gives you an understanding of your approach and how you want to handle the circumstances.

Toward the end of my time at John Frieda, there was a walk out. There were talks of people leaving John Frieda and going to the Sally Hershberger Salon. I was torn because I wanted to be part of a team. At the same time, I saw there was room for me to accomplish a few goals while in this position. This rumor was major. It was interesting to watch the behavior of those who were leaving in comparison to those who stayed. The team of people going outnumbered those staying. I had to ignore all of the secrets, the whispering and awkward public conversations.

My purpose for getting a job at John Frieda was to earn my apprenticeship, get my license, and earn my chair on the floor.

I was aware enough of my purpose and goals, as well as the opportunities that laid before me to avoid the chaos. Because of this awareness and dedicated focus, I maintained and accomplished my goals.

STAY FOCUSED

To take your awareness even further, you must be able to discern when it's appropriate for you to engage in conversations. Moreover, determine when it'll be detrimental and distracting to your job.

In the beginning, it's natural to talk when we are comfortable or looking to gain favor. We tend to become more verbally expressive than normal. It's understandable to be reactive when you are really excited, since it is normal to want to be liked.

Most new assistants want to jump right in, letting everyone know just how smart and talented they are. I must caution you against doing this. Instead of telling what you think you know, focus on what you are going to learn. Focus on understanding the process before you add the extra conversation.

When working on set for any project, your focus should be a hundred percent on the key and a hundred percent on the talent. I don't know how that is possible, but it is. Remember, this is amazing opportunity with a hands-on instructor. So, you should behave as if this was your last job ever.

Don't let yourself get distracted.

In this day and age, there are lots of distractions which can completely sidetrack you and throw your focus off course. There have been times when my attention was challenged by a new environment, new people, first time jitters working with someone, notifications buzzing on my phone, or getting lost in my own thoughts. There'll be times when your attention is needed, but the circumstances of life keep your thoughts tied up. Your body is present but your mind is miles away. This means the person with whom you are working has to stop their flow to get your attention. You can really slow up the process, thereby causing a distraction to the key.

When you show that you can be easily distracted, you come across as disinterested, and unprofessional. I had to learn to ignore all the things around me. When I am working, I have learned to put on blinders and focus only on the job at hand.

Your focus will allow you to avoid drastic mistakes.

Being around celebrities for the first time can be overwhelming. Focusing on what you are doing can be nerve-wracking and intimidating as you work with several media cameramen. Yet, with all these things going on around you, you must not allow your focus to slip.

I can remember the moment this lesson set in for me. I was working New York Fashion Week with Orlando Pita, hired to style the Carolina Herrrera Fashion Show. I was extremely new to the process and the environment. I needed Orlando's help to complete the look on a model due to my execution not being on point.

Fortunately, I was aware enough to realize what the artist needed. And, I was humble enough to ask for his direction. When Orlando came to my station, I wasn't prepared for what happened. As we started working with the model, I could see ten photographers out of the corner of my eye. They were taking pictures of what we were doing. This look required both of my hands and eyes to make it work. I had to ignore everything that was happening around me. I couldn't react to anything that wasn't involved with completing the look successfully. My attention was only tuned into what Orlando needed of me. If I had chosen to do anything other than this, I would've blown my opportunity to work in this industry, abruptly ending the beginning of a long-standing work relationship.

The next morning, I received a text from a very close friend. There was a picture of me and Orlando Pita on Glamour Magazine's social media pages. The picture was a highlight of my career. However, I can only imagine the disaster that picture would have been if the cameras caught me in a stare of distraction.

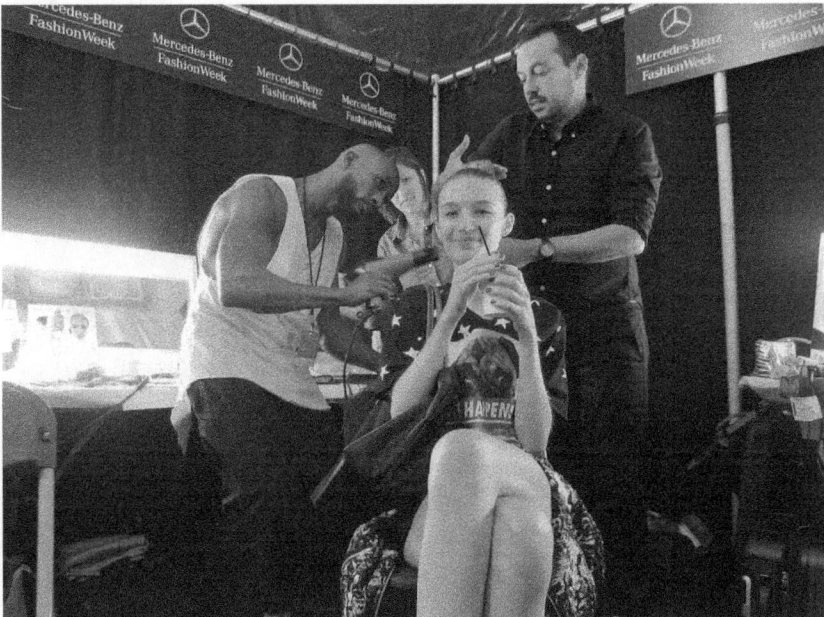

STAMINA

GRIT IS THAT 'EXTRA SOMETHING' THAT SEPARATES THE MOST SUCCESSFUL PEOPLE FROM THE REST. IT'S THE PASSION, PERSEVERANCE, AND STAMINA THAT WE MUST CHANNEL IN ORDER TO STICK WITH OUR DREAMS UNTIL THEY BECOME A REALITY.

TRAVIS BRADBERRY

IImagine this: you've reached your goal of becoming a professional assistant in the entertainment industry. You're assisting on editorials and campaigns for celebrity clients of your dreams.

You might think that you have it made. You're in the door and it's smooth sailing from here on, right?

Well, here's the truth—the hard work is just beginning. If you don't develop the stamina and mental fortitude of an athlete, then you're not going to be able to stay in the industry for long. Like a professional athlete, your talent and ability are not enough. You must thrive on your tenacity, endurance, and commitment to push beyond your limits.

Physical Stamina

The hours are long. The work is grueling. The expectations are high, and always changing. You must be in tip top condition, ready for peak performance at all times.

Upon first entering the industry, I was simply not prepared to handle the level of sheer exertion and effort. Not only was I working ten to twelve hours a day, but those hours were filled with activity. There was no standing around and shooting the breeze. Many people crave being behind the scenes in the entertainment industry, thinking they will have lots of free time to hobnob and rub elbows with famous people. There's no time for that!

Your stamina will be tested on many levels, no matter your job. There'll be times you may need to run an errand at an odd hour, survive extreme weather conditions, carry multiple large suitcases, or run from the set to the client's trailer multiple times. This is all in addition to the work you've been hired to do. As an assistant, your tasks are unlimited.

When your energy becomes fatigued, your integrity gets tested and the quality of your work could go down the drain. We don't want that to happen, do we?

That's why it is important to keep yourself in the best shape possible. You want to look fresh and able to handle whatever comes your way, even if you just carried several suitcases up four flights of stairs or lugged a lighting kit three miles down the beach. When you are in proper physical condition, your senses are sharp. This, in turn, shows in your effectiveness and efficiency on the job. I have found that, when I am in my best shape, my work ability is heightened.

REMINDER: This is not your typical 9 to 5

I've said it before, and I'll say it again: you will have long hours. Ten-to-twelve-hour workdays are not unusual. As your client's first line of offense and last line of defense, you'll often be the first person to arrive in your department and the last one to leave.

Dealing With The Night Before Jitters

One thing that has the ability to seriously affect your stamina is the Night Before Jitters. The night before a big event or shoot can be hell. No matter how much you've prepared and planned, things pop up at the last minute that you have to handle. Often you are up late into the night ensuring everything is ready for the next day. When everything is finally in place, you have only a few hours to rest and recharge.

Only, you can't sleep.

Eyes wide open staring at the ceiling, your mind is racing.

Did I do everything I was supposed to do?

What about...?

What if...?

And then, there comes the real pressure: what if I oversleep? The competition is fierce and being late is a huge faux pas. If I mess up, even once, I could lose my position. With all of these thoughts swirling through your mind, you toss and turn, waking up every hour until the alarm clock sounds. Due to a restless night, you're more exhausted than you were when you laid down.

This happens to all professional assistants. No matter how long you've been in the industry, there will be nights like this. Your stamina will be your best friend on these days.

Here's my advice to you —

Before the event, store up as much energy as you can.

Unfortunately, this is not a place where I'll cut you any slack. You've got to be on top of your game no matter how much, or how little, sleep you had the night before a big event. When you are supporting someone else, it's your job to make sure the deliverables are met and things run smoothly throughout the day. If you don't do your part, it not only affects your client; the entire project is affected as well.

Emotional Stamina

In life, there are always moments that will push your emotional boundaries. In an industry of creatives and egos, this won't be the time to be sensitive in any fashion. It took some time for me to develop a tough enough skin to not be affected by the things I cannot control.

That's the key to developing and maintaining emotional stamina. Learn the difference between the things you can control and the things you can't. Things such as the emotional states, opinions, attitudes, thoughts, and behaviors of others are things you simply cannot control. What someone else thinks about you is none of your concern. Let them handle their own toxic and negative energy.

You also can't control your past. There'll be times when you make a mistake. There'll be times when things that normally work will fail. That's life. Things happen—and sometimes, they happen at the worst possible time.

The key to maintaining your emotional stamina in these situations is to get over it quickly.

Don't wallow in self-pity or blame. As soon as the events happen, they're in the past. You can't change the past once it has happened. Instead, focus on the present and how you can make new decisions to have a better future. Remember, you're in control of your own emotions, attitudes, behaviors, and thoughts. Choose to remain positive and focused on your goals.

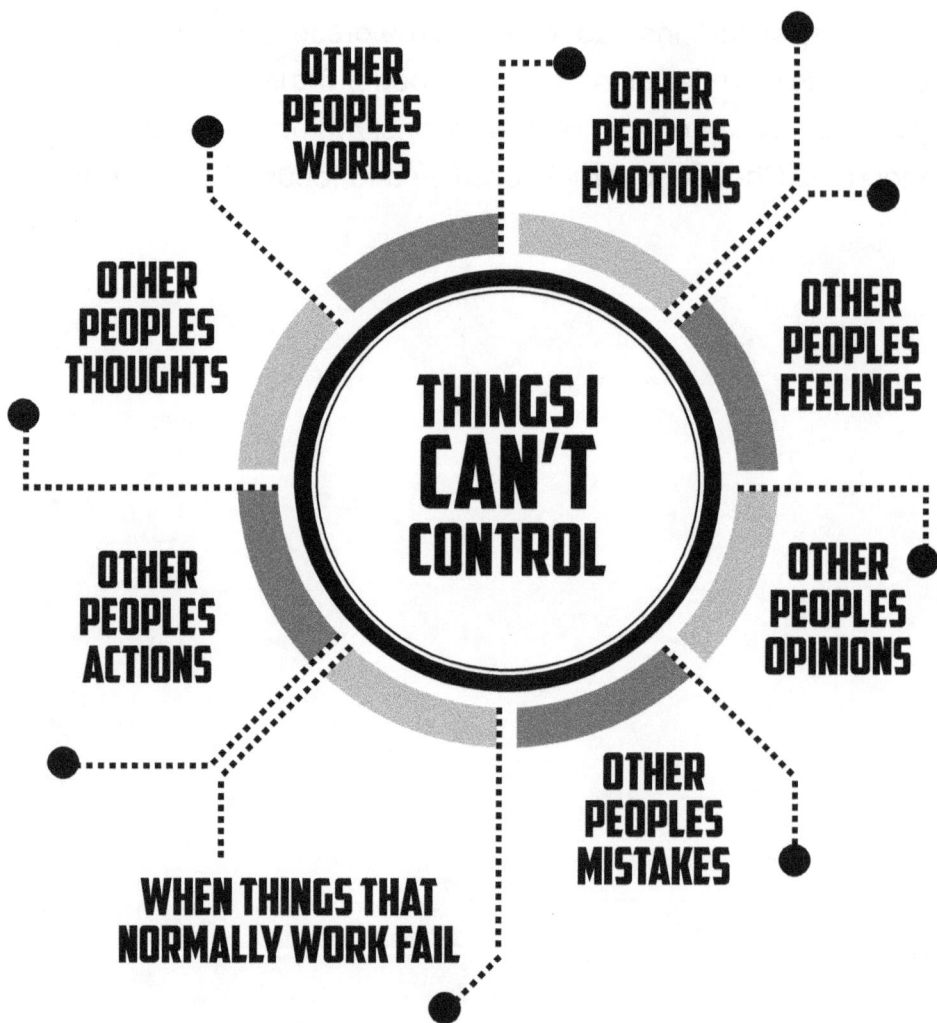

THINGS I CAN'T CONTROL

- OTHER PEOPLES WORDS
- OTHER PEOPLES EMOTIONS
- OTHER PEOPLES FEELINGS
- OTHER PEOPLES OPINIONS
- OTHER PEOPLES MISTAKES
- WHEN THINGS THAT NORMALLY WORK FAIL
- OTHER PEOPLES ACTIONS
- OTHER PEOPLES THOUGHTS

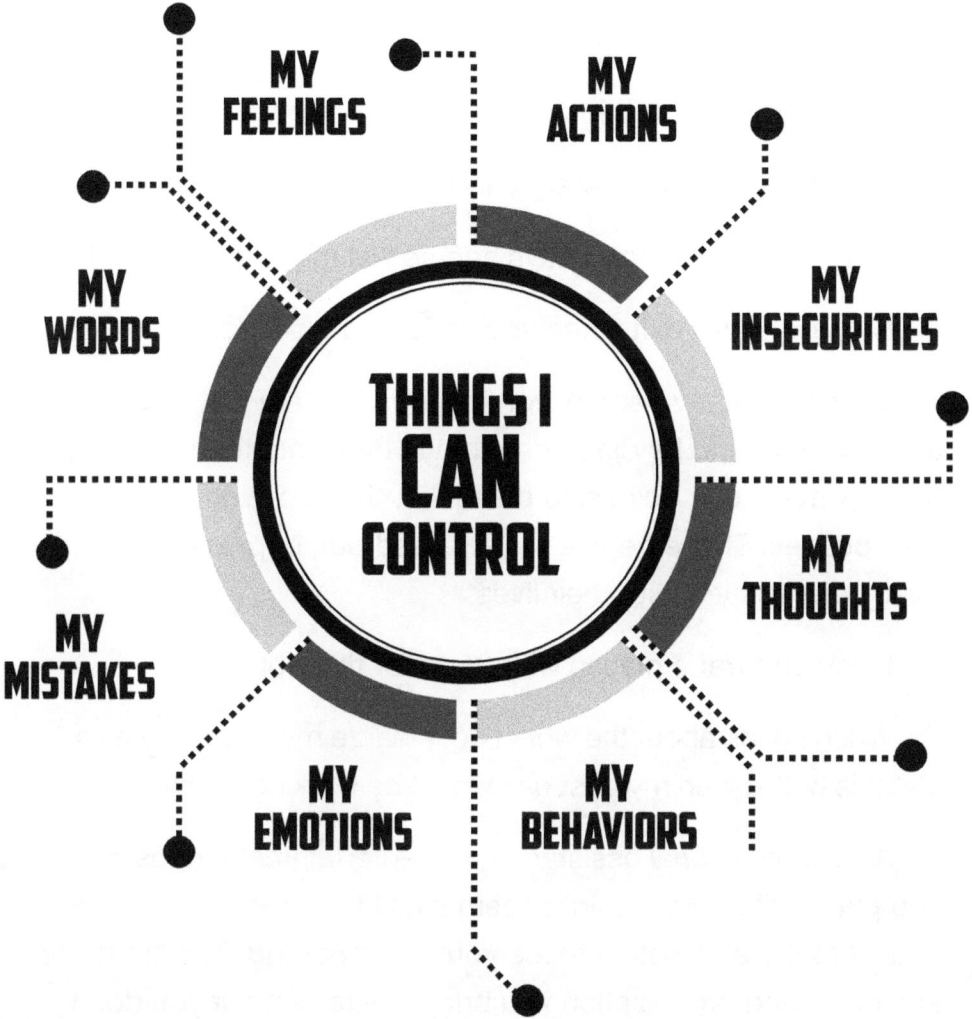

MY
FEELINGS

MY
ACTIONS

MY
WORDS

MY
INSECURITIES

THINGS I
CAN
CONTROL

MY
THOUGHTS

MY
MISTAKES

MY
EMOTIONS

MY
BEHAVIORS

"You Have To Love It" - Teddy Charles

After reading this chapter, you might be thinking, "Why would anyone want to put up with this?"

The answer is: "You've got to love it."

Yes, being a professional assistant is hard work.

Yes, it takes a lot of energy and endurance.

Yes, there will be long days and sometimes long nights, too.

But, it's all worth it when you are doing work you love.

There are many people working jobs that are just as arduous and demanding. The difference that is they hate them. They go to work every day despising their jobs, their co-workers, and their bosses. These people are stressed out, depressed, and overly dissatisfied with their lives.

I wouldn't trade places with them for the world!

When I think about the work I do, I realize my worst day as a stylist is better than my best day would be working in any other job.

As a professional assistant in the entertainment industry, you play a vital role. It might seem small to some, but you are critical to the success of those you're supporting. The creativity, ingenuity, and organization you bring is vital. And, if you don't love what you do, your work will suffer.

Will there be times when you get frustrated and think about giving it all up? Of course.

In those times, go back to your goals and dreams. Remember why you started.

In fact, that's probably a good thing for you to do right now. Go back to the place where you wrote down your desires. Read your reasons for pursuing a career as a professional assistant. Keep this vision in your mind at all times. It will keep you focused and motivated, so you are able to push through when the going gets tough.

BE A CUT ABOVE THE REST

Maintaining a high standard

Stand out. There is nothing new under the sun, but by maintaining your standards of service, you stand out. While assisting, you should have high standards and expectations of yourself and processes. If you are organized, be extremely organized. Always look to raise the bar of how you operate.

Maintaining a high level of efficiency will never be overlooked or underrated.

Make a conscious effort.

It's important that you're making decisions that have been thought through. Always look to improve the current work situation. You will have to pay attention to every derail. Intuition with any stylist will develop through time and experience.

Set Yourself up for success

Maintaining a high standard of integrity is vitally important. Competition is high and people talk. My grandfather once told me all we have in this world is our word. In this industry, work ethic reputation is everything. The type of work with which you are associated follows you everywhere. You'll have to prove you are willing and ready to work harder than the last time. You want everyone to know that you get what is going on and have full confidence in your ability.

My first opportunity to be an assistant for an editorial shoot was with Ashley Javier. The agent told me that it was going to be challenging, but if I worked out for him, other opportunities could open up in the future. I had no Idea that for which I was in store. It was a day I would never forget.

Because of that experience, I committed myself to be a specific type of assistant. I was committed to focusing on the key, along with their every move and process. I was committed to the point of becoming intuitive. After watching someone go through their process, I would try to prepare them for the next step. I knew I wasn't just working for this job; I was building my reputation for the jobs that would come next.

People who make the effort to refer you must be able to trust your level of work. They want to know you won't make them look bad.

Your conscious effort will become intuitive through repetition. But this effect will be noticed right away to the person you are assisting. As a professional, you'll develop a flow and process that allows your work to be successful.

Make yourself essential

You've landed one opportunity of a lifetime. Now what? How do you continue to get booked for even more great opportunities? The answer: make yourself essential to any team by working your ass off. Hard work is visible and rewardable.

After my first experience working on set, I had the electric elite hairstylist feeling and I wanted more. I wasn't getting the set jobs often, but when I did, I focused on bringing my strengths to the table. I wanted the agency to hire me again. So, I was extra attentive, quick and respectful.

Integrity

I must remind you: Your reputation will precede you! It's important that you represent yourself well at all times. It's necessary that you hold a spot for integrity as the foundation of your career. Your integrity can be proven by being reliable, hardworking, dedicated, and committed. As an assistant, your trust is mandatory. Your ability to make decisions in the client's best interest is a must.

Sometimes your tasks may seem trivial, but you're there to make things happen.

No one likes lazy or slow. Being a labeled as a handworker is an asset to any team. When a hard work ethic is recognized, you'll get more opportunities. A good work ethic on a team can push through a day of mishaps and delays. Always stay ready and willing to get the task done, no matter what the time or what has to be done next.

There have been times when I was tired, cold, and ready to go. Still, there was more to be done. For whatever reason, there is a hold up. You have to finish strong, and not give up when your fatigue settles in.

The worst fatigue for me was doing blow-dries...

Working at a MYBLOW LA, I would get girls with insane amounts of hair who wanted that blowout of the year. Halfway through the blow out, I'd be ready to put it down. I would lose the amount of normal tension I would use. The hair wouldn't have the same shine and finish. I had to tell myself to finish strong and not give up on the blow dry! When I was tired and almost at the breaking point, I'd encourage myself to push through. It might sound like a small matter but that's how you must approach every job. Big or small. You must give a hundred percent of your effort every time.

EARNING RESPECT AND PROVING YOUR PASSION

In the beginning of my journey as a professional assistant, I'd ask myself or anyone that I knew, "How do I become a celebrity hairstylist or fashion hair stylist?"

I'd take any opportunity I could to assist under someone who might have any knowledge. Assisting was a test of my will, whereby I could learn and achieve my goals. It was hard to deal with other people's issues, trying to get to know them and be supportive while honing my craft. It seemed as if each person I assisted required me to prove myself over and over again.

I had to prove that I was dedicated to the job and consistent. As time went on, I knew I wanted my reputation to be stellar. So, I put in the effort to better myself and my craft. I knew what my strong points were and when it was time to step my game up.

I'd copy the techniques of each person I assisted.

I may not have had all the tools or hair products, but I'd practice what I saw that day. This allowed me to internalize and digest what I learned. Each time I showed up, I'd stronger knowledge and was a little more capable.

As I learned what to do, I also learned what not to do. I carefully observed the behaviors of other stylists, while seeing many things I didn't want to repeat.

There were times I assisted artists who treated me in ways that I wouldn't deal with in my personal life. But due to the delicate circumstances, I bit my tongue off, put it in a Fed-Ed box and shipped it across the country, just so I could keep my job and advance my career.

I reached many milestones as a professional assistant because I put the emotions aside and dealt with what I wanted out of each experience. I was determined not to let anyone get in the way of that, directly or indirectly. I stayed the course. Even when the course changed, I was flexible, just to keep a foot in the door.

After eight years of working in Los Angeles—reflecting on the people with whom I've worked—here's one thing I know for sure:

Respect is earned and your passion is proven over time.

The respect you receive from others in the industry will be hard earned. It'll come when people see you for a while. realizing that you are still working and living your dream. My father would tell me that if you ever feel as if you're not moving in life, look back on the last six months. Reflect on what has happened. If nothing has happened, there's your answer. However, it's time to push for more if you recognize the growth and changes which have happened on your journey.

In the beginning of my journey, I'd often say, "I can't wait 'til I am at this point in my career." Envisioning myself on a trajectory of rapid growth, I saw where I wanted to go but didn't know how to get there. I knew I had a lot to learn; I was completely new this industry. I learned to be present with my experiences. It only happens once and it's completely up to you to get what you want out of it. I knew that there was lots for me to learn and explore, but it took time. Just like anyone else, I wanted life to happen fast and better like the person next to me. I learned that this journey is a marathon, instead of a 200-yard dash.

Failure

Even though we believe in ourselves, and we believe that we can do anything, sometimes we have to realize that failure will happen. In fact, I believe failing can be the best thing that happens to an assistant at times.

It's understood that, as a professional, you want all jobs to go without a problem. You will do anything in your power to make things work. However, things can happen that are out of your control. Even with your best foot forward, things don't always work the way you intended. Please hold your head up, take a deep breath, and try again. Don't lie down in self-pity or reflection. If you are truly passionate, you'll take the time to make those changes in your approach.

No one wants to be a failure, but these are also opportunities. We learn from our mistakes, proving to ourselves that we can grow and develop regardless of our circumstances.

While assisting at John Frieda, I had the chance to assist Serge Normant for a John Frieda commercial in Los Angeles. I was extremely nervous and new at being on set assisting. So, I was very stiff and eager to make things work.

The first day went well. Since it was a two-day shoot, I offered to take Serge's kit to the location for the second day.

After wrapping, I headed to my second job. I was moonlighting as bathroom security at the Troubador. The hours were brutal: eight p.m. to three a.m. But I had to do it. I needed the money because, at the time, assisting in the salon only paid eight dollars an hour.

As the night went on, I knew I wasn't feeling good. I made it through the night, knowing I did not have much time to rest before the shoot. The next morning, with only a couple hours of rest and flu like symptoms, I woke up...fifteen minutes late! As a result, I was late getting to the location with Serge's kit.

He was kind to me, considering the circumstance in which I put him. Needless to say, I felt crushed. I'd let myself down. I felt and thought that I would never work on set ever again.

It took me a few days to get over it. After a good pity party, I decided to turn my mistake into a learning experience. I made changes in my plan that better aligned with my goals. I changed the way I looked at the outcome, focusing on how I could improve. I made a commitment to myself that I would not let opportunities outside of hair interfere with my career in the hair industry. From that point forward, I decided to only take side jobs that aligned with my career. I didn't have a set schedule for my salon work and I needed to be available to work freelance gigs. So, I focused on creating a flow of supplemental income by taking house calls to my friends and new clients.

The lesson for me was to not lay down in your mistakes and over think what and why. That becomes a vicious cycle.

Whether or not I was ever going to work with Serge or in the industry again, I didn't give up. I chose to get back in the game mentally by preparing myself for the next opportunity.

Your passion will be observed through your dedication and body of work. The respect of your peers also comes with dedication and commitment to your journey. Relax, recognize, relate and enjoy the process of your development. Learning from your mistakes can be fun, depending on how you want to look at things.

PERSONALIZE YOUR RELATIONSHIPS

In the beginning of my career, I realized that it's important to have the right relationships with the right people. I've always had long-term plans and goals for my success. So, I would keep all business cards and information that I collected– even if I wasn't always sure what role a person could play in my success. At the time of collecting cards, I didn't think of it as data collecting; but over time, having this information gave me a huge resource.

As you build your own relationships, here are some things to keep in mind—

- **Everyone is a resource.** People come in and out of our lives for a purpose. It's up to us to discover what that purpose is.

- **Developing relationships takes time and timing.** The road to success is a marathon. Therefore, you are going to have to be patient and trust the process.

The trust, which involves tearing down any barrier, will take several interactions with each other. I have observed that, the more moments someone has had with you, whether good or bad, you are able to establish a level of predictability within that scenario. In time and through your conversations, you'll increase and have context.

STOP THE EXCUSES

EXCUSES ARE THE FASTEST WAY AWAY FROM AN OPPORTUNITY!

Excuses are the primary reason most professional assistants fail to accomplish the success they desire to have throughout the entertainment industry. There'll always be a circumstance for which you can blame someone else. Mediocre assistants come up with all kinds of reasons as to why they can't handle a particular job, why they're running behind schedule, and/or why they just couldn't exercise self-control. There's always a reason why. The majority of the time, that reason has nothing to do with them or you.

If you want to rise above the crowd, thereby setting yourself apart as a highly qualified and valuable professional assistant, one of the most important habits you can build is to make a proactive commitment. Furthermore, stop making excuses.

You'll have to accept responsibility for whatever task is at hand. This might involve being on time, having the right tools for the job, or any short coming that could happen. Understand that no one cares about why your execution falls short. It's not that the industry is just cold and really couldn't care less about your life. While that is certainly true at times, the reasons go far beyond that.

When you constantly make excuses for poor, lackluster performance, you show those around you that you are:

- **Not serious about your job or craft;**

- **Self-centered or more focused on your own comfort over the success of your client or the project on which you are working;**

- **Uncertain about your own skill level or ability;**

- **Unwilling to accept responsibility; and/or**

- **Not motivated to step outside of your comfort zone, so that you can grow and improve.**

Here is something important for you to consider— there are people dealing with the same, or even worse, circumstances as you do. Still, they're able to get the job done. There's someone living farther from the job site than you do, having twice as long of a commute in heavy traffic. Though, they still manage to make it to work half an hour early. There're people who got less sleep than you did the night before, but they still come to work with a great attitude.

Bottom line: life happens. Circumstances come up.

People make mistakes.

I find that a person's determination can conquer any obstacle. When we decide to set our mind to a goal, we can and will stop at nothing. What's important is that you don't just allow a situation to be a problem. It is your job to find a solution and make things happen—no matter what.

Leave off the "but"

Most people have way too many buts.

I'm sorry I'm late, but traffic was insane.

I'm sorry that I don't have the right tools for the job, but no one told me exactly what we'd be doing today.

I'm sorry I lost my temper, but he just pushed all the wrong buttons.

When you make a mistake, own up to it. Don't try to rationalize your shortcomings with excuses, blaming other people or circumstances. This only shows people that you are not a true professional. Simply apologize and move on. When you make excuses and/or blame others, you're not taking the proper responsibility. Ultimately, you'll likely not learn from your mistakes and do it over again...and again.

Confronting Your Excuses

What are your most common excuses? For example – I'm often late because...; I'm unprepared for my workday because...; I don't have enough time to finish because...

Reflect upon yourself, noting the most common excuses which you give to everyday circumstances in your control. These excuses are behaviors that we develop and adopt as our natural behavior. You can bring awareness to what your behavior patterns are, thereby developing a resolution through which to correct them.

Here is a great exercise you can do which will help rid yourself of your excuses.

Think about the areas of your professional life where you regularly make excuses. Write them down. Examine the reasons behind why you make excuses for each listed area. Honestly assess each excuse to determine your responsibility. Write down at least three things which helps you change each excuse to excellent behavior.

Think about the areas of your professional life where you regularly make excuses. Write them down. For each area listed, examine the reasons behind the excuse. Honestly assess each excuse to determine your responsibility. Write down at least three things you can do to change each excuse into excellent behavior.

WORK HARD, PLAY HARDER, AND LOVE YOURSELF MORE!

Work Hard

YOU GET WHAT YOUR WORK FOR, NOT WHAT YOU WISH FOR.

As a growing, ambitious assistant, hard work is at the core of your success. You must be willing to put in the time, effort, and energy to propel yourself to the top of your game.

Many assistants believe that the hard work to which you commit starts and ends on set. However, I'm here to tell you differently. The work you do does not stop when the shoot or the show is over. That's when your work is just beginning. The real hard work of being a professional assistant comes in up leveling your skills to constantly seek growth and improvement. Whether you're just observing a haircut or assisting on set, always find an opportunity to study your craft.

I use everyday situations as my classroom. As I'm out in various settings, I observe people, doing quick consultations. I first observe what they are wearing and how they styled their hair. You can learn about how the haircut grows out and what you would do differently. Hint: In our everyday life, there're opportunities for us to observe and make suggestions for how to apply, fix, and/or handle a circumstance in our profession. So, it's vital to be sharp and prepared.

Play Harder

BY WORKING HARD
YOU GET TO PLAY HARDER—GUILT FREE.

If you put in the hard work, it'll pay off. And, the great news is—your play time will pay off too.

Don't spend all of your time working. If you do, you'll not only be overly stressed and quickly burned out, but you will also miss out on many opportunities to advance your career.

How can playing harder help me advance my career, you ask?

Well, it's all about being a well-rounded person. We don't work alone. We work with other people. One of our most basic human needs is to socialize and connect with others. As you connect with others, they come to know, like, and trust you.

Guess what happens when people know, like, and trust you? They look out for you. They keep you in mind when new opportunities arise. They recommend you to others.

So, enjoy your time away from work. Socialize. Connect with your community.

Love Yourself More

IT'S NOT SELFISH TO LOVE YOURSELF, TAKE CARE OF YOURSELF, AND MAKE YOUR HAPPINESS A PRIORITY. IT'S NECESSARY.
WENDY HALE

We take care of people every day. It's our job and we love doing it. However, you must not forget that your most important client is you. In order to take care of others, you must first take care of yourself.

The better you take care of yourself, the better you will be able to take care of others. Here are a few self-care tips every professional assistant should keep in mind.

- **Dress for Success.** Looking good on the outside reflects how you feel about yourself on the inside. Taking pride in your grooming and personal appearance will give you a boost of confidence, therefore showing that you make yourself a priority.

- **Stay sharp mentally.** Most people will focus on exercise, diet, relaxation, and sleep as their top self-care tips. While these are great, perhaps more important is your mental health. Laughter, meditation, learning something new, journaling, and spending time outside are great ways to keep yourself mentally healthy.

- **Establish a daily self-care routine.** Put it on your calendar and make an appointment. At least one hour of everyday should be devoted to you. Whether you spend the time leisurely reading or going for a run, do something each day that's only about you.

CLEAR COMMUNICATION AND TRANSPARENCY

Professional assistants are super planners. We have to be. We handle a multitude of challenging and conflicting tasks, schedules, and personalities every day without breaking a sweat.

But, it's only in an ideal world that all things always go as planned. No matter how perfectly prepared you are, things happen. Circumstances change. Situations beyond your control show up.

How do you handle it?

With clear communication, transparency, and a smile.

Here's my advice on how to deal with unexpected circumstances:

1. **Take a deep breath and calm down.**
   You won't be any good to your client if you go into panic mode. Breathing deeply will clear your mind, allowing you to think with clarity and focus.

2. **Step back and evaluate the situation.**
   Once your mind is clear, you will be able to fully examine the situation and determine the best next steps. Ask yourself:

   • What is the problem? What is the goal or expected outcome?

   • What is the current situation?

- What resources do you have at your disposal in this moment?

- Who can help you in this situation?

- What is the best possible solution? Are there other solutions available?

Most importantly, answer the last question. Never take an issue to your client without also taking solutions.

3. **Clearly communicate with your client.**
   As soon as you have a good grasp of the situation and possible solutions, inform your client. Be clear in your communication, telling your client exactly what has happened. Moreover, clarify your plan toward addressing the issue. As you communicate with your client, keep the following advice in mind:

   - Be up front with your client. Explain the situation precisely with as much detail as possible.

   - Don't pass blame or make excuses. Stick to the facts and the solution.

   - Keep your cool. Remain calm. Your composure during difficult and unexpected situations will put your client at ease. You'll receive a deeper level of respect and trust, and your client will be comfortable allowing you to handle more decisions in the future.

4. **Don't vent about the situation**.

   When frustrating situations arise, it can be tempting to complain and vent about them to others. Don't do this! Not only will you be in jeopardy of betraying your client's confidence, but you'll also be seen as a whiny crybaby. You'll lose the respect of your client and others in the industry.

GREAT ENERGY

Have you heard the saying, "Your attitude determines your altitude?" Well, I have a saying of my own—Your energy determines everything.

Your energy—that invisible force field surrounding you—is a powerful tool that can be used for good or for evil. Energy has the ability not only to affect your own attitude, emotions, thoughts, and behavior. It can also affect the attitudes, emotions, thoughts, and behaviors of those around you.

Imagine this: you're preparing your client for a big photo shoot. The stakes are high—this is a really important deal. Your client is nervous and agitated, maybe even a bit snappy.

The client's aggravation has rubbed off on the photographer and other members of the crew. Everyone is on edge. Noticing the dark cloud hanging over the room, you put a big smile on your face and project a calm energy into the room. Instead of snapping back or getting frustrated, you radiate positivity. Your calm, positive energy is reflected in your tone of voice and the confidence in your work. Soon, your energy spreads throughout the room. Your client begins to settle down. The photographer brightens up. The crew becomes more productive. Soon, the entire room Is buzzing with positive energy.

Energies are infectious, and your energy can change everything!

That's why the greatest trait a professional assistant can cultivate is the ability to maintain great energy.

You might be reading this and thinking, "That's great for those happy all the time people but having great energy just doesn't come naturally to me."

The great news is—you don't have to be born with great energy. You can learn how to create and keep positive energy around you. All it takes is a little effort and intention. Trust me. It will be worth it. Once you learn how to give off a more positive energy, the world will be your oyster.

Here's why: like attracts like.

The energy you put off shapes the reality of the environment around you. If your energy is negative, the circumstances around you will appear negative as well. However, when your energy is positive, the circumstances around you will be positive. So, the more positive energy you project, the better you will think, act, and feel. And, the better you think, act, and feel, then the better those around you will think, act and feel. The better people around you think, act, and feel, then the more amazing opportunities are created. New doors will be opened for you and your life will be elevated beyond your belief.

Don't believe me? Think about it for a moment. Who seems to get all of the big breaks? Who are those people who always seem to have the best opportunities? Who are the people in your field who always seem to have all the luck and always come out on top?

It's the people with the most positive energy.

Why? We are in the people business. And, people like to work with fun, engaging, and positive people who brighten their day. These people make work enjoyable. They don't like to work with mean-spirited, energy vampires who sap the energy out of life.

Don't get me wrong. I'm not telling you that you have to be cheerful twenty-four hours a day, or seven days a week. That is impossible. There'll be times when your energy is low, and you're just having a bad day. That's called life. The key is to learn how to tap into your positive vibes when you need them most.

Look For The Silver Lining

"FIND THE MIRACLE IN YOUR DAY."
SHACOLE HAMLETT

Don't dwell on the negative in a situation. Even when bad things happen, it's your reaction to those bad things that matters most. If you choose to play the role of a victim, complaining and blaming others, the negativity of the situation will be magnified. When circumstances arise that challenge your energy, here's what to do:

- **Stop talking about the situation in a negative way as if there is nothing you can do about it. Don't feed into the negative energy.**

- **• Find the blessings and lessons in the situation. You've heard it before: every cloud has a silver lining. In every situation, no matter how bad it may seem, there is something positive if you choose to look for it.**

Don't Be Too Hard On Yourself

The entertainment industry is built on portraying images of perfection. On television and movie screens, on the covers of magazines or the fashion runways – we're great at making everything look flawless. But as a professional assistant, you know that things are far from perfect. Those images on the screen have been filtered. Touch ups have been done to cover photos, and those clothes models wear while walking down the runway are being held together by duct tape. You know everything is not perfect in the entertainment industry, so why do you think you have to be?

Your inner critic will create more negativity than any external situation ever could. More times than not, the negative energy people put out into the world stems from their own negative thoughts about themselves. Those thoughts turn into internal words of criticism and that internal criticism turns into negative behavior towards others.

Feeding The Situation

Stop feeding the situation with energy, thoughts, or attention. Instead of criticizing yourself for what you think you are not, honor and embrace who you are. When you find yourself saying or thinking something critical about you, immediately say five things that are positive about yourself. The more you do this, the more your confidence and sense of self-worth will increase. Moreover, the positive energy you have will radiate.

Immediate Energy Boosters

The tips I've shared with you so far will work when it comes to cultivating a positive energy on a long-term basis. But, what happens if you find yourself in a situation where you need an immediate energy boost? Here are some tricks you can use in the moment when you must go from negative to positive in an instant.

- **Stop Complaining. Start Problem Solving.** Project running behind schedule? Client overly agitated? Things just not going the way you planned? It's normal to get upset, frustrated, or even angry in these situations.

  However, giving in to these emotions will take you on a downward spiral toward negativity. Instead, take it as an opportunity to showcase your brilliant problem-solving skills. Turn the negative problem into a positive solution. Immediately take five minutes to brainstorm possible solutions once you notice a problem. As the solutions flow, your positive energy will be enhanced.

- **Get Moving.** The negativity you are feeling needs some kind of release. Movement is a natural energy booster. As soon as you start moving, oxygen-rich blood pumps throughout your body to your heart, muscles, and brain. A simple five-minute walk will help you blow off steam and get the positive energy flowing.

Knowing What You Want

> # "I DON'T CARE HOW MUCH POWER, BRILLIANCE, OR ENERGY YOU HAVE. IF YOU DON'T HARNESS IT AND FOCUS IT ON A SPECIFIC TARGET, AND HOLD IT THERE YOU ARE NEVER GOING TO ACCOMPLISH AS MUCH AS YOUR ABILITY WARRANTS. "
> ### ZIG ZIGLAR

We all want more out of our lives. We desire to do meaningful work that leads to greater success, happiness, and wealth. On top of all that, we also want to enjoy our lives. Attaining this higher level of success requires two key factors: a clear direction and a solid foundation.

A Clear Direction

Would you go on a cross country trip without your GPS giving you the right directions? Of course not! These days, we don't even go across town without turning on our GPS. Why, then, would you try to navigate your way to the success of your dreams without a roadmap?

Having a clear direction ensures you don't get lost along the way. It saves you a lot of time, money, and energy. Likewise, it saves you all of the frustration and overwhelm which you want to avoid.

Just as you would use a GPS on a cross country trip, the first step to determining your direction for success is to know exactly where you're going. The more exact and specific you are, the easier it is to plot your course.

What's Your Direction?

In the space below (or in your journal), clearly describe your goals and desires. What do you want your career to look like? With whom would you like to work? What lifestyle would you like to enjoy?

A Solid Foundation

Not only do you need to know where you are going, but you also need to know why you want to go there. In many cases, the why is equally if not more important than the where.

Why do you want to be on this path?

This is a critical question to ask yourself. The answer will serve as the foundational guidepost for your journey. As with everything else in life, there will be moments of uncertainty. You'll come to certain places along your journey where you have to make decisions which affect your course. Some decisions will help you to stay on track, while others will create detours. Essentially these detours make your journey longer and a lot more difficult.

The entertainment industry is filled with glitzy and glamourous opportunities. Many times these opportunities look great, but this is not the case if they are not aligned with your goals or intentions.

What's Your Foundation?

In the space provided below (or in your journal), clearly answer this question: Why do you want to be an assistant in the entertainment industry?

CLOSING

I wrote this handbook with the new assistant in mind. I wrote it to be simple and straightforward. You don't need a bunch of complex and convoluted set of instructions.

From my years of experience as a personal assistant, I know it isn't always easy. I know it's hard to get people to open up and tell you what it really takes to succeed. I hope that, by reading this book, you will have a clearer picture.

The main points to keep in mind are:

- Maintain your passion

- Stay focused and persistent

- Build your stamina

- Keep learning and growing

- Earn respect

- Operate in integrity

- Make no excuses

- Know what you want

I believe you can do anything. You can excel when you are to make the changes, thereby becoming the best version of yourself. I wish you all the success you desire!

www.ingramcontent.com/pod-product-compliance
Lightning Source LLC
Chambersburg PA
CBHW022051190326
41520CB00008B/772